WEST VIRGINIA

Past and Present

Ann Byers

rosen publishing's
rosen central

New York

Published in 2011 by The Rosen Publishing Group, Inc.
29 East 21st Street, New York, NY 10010

Library of Congress Cataloging-in-Publication Data

Byers, Ann.
West Virginia: past and present / Ann Byers.— 1st ed.
        p. cm. — (The United States: past and present)
Includes bibliographical references and index.
ISBN 978-1-4358-9499-0 (library binding)
ISBN 978-1-4358-9526-3 (pbk.)
ISBN 978-1-4358-9560-7 (6-pack)
1. West Virginia—Juvenile literature. I. Title.
F241.3.B94 2011
975.4—dc22

                                                                    2010002514

Manufactured in Malaysia

CPSIA Compliance Information: Batch #S10YA: For further information, contact Rosen Publishing, New York, New York, at 1-800-237-9932.

On the cover: Top left: A print of Harpers Ferry by Currier and Ives. Top right: A loaded coal barge is pushed along the Kanawha River. Bottom: The Blackwater Falls in the hills of West Virginia.

Contents

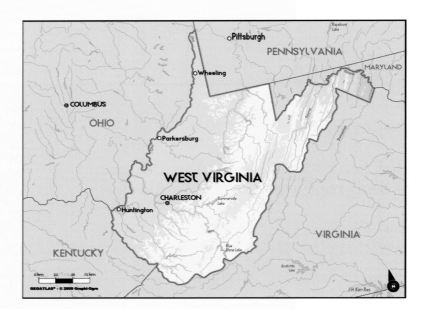

Tucked between four states, West Virginia is at the northern edge of the South Atlantic states. It is oval in shape with one panhandle jutting north and another stretching northeast.

Introduction

The Mountain State is aptly named. Nearly everything about West Virginia is defined by its mountains. Most of its boundaries are formed by rivers that originate in the highlands. Its history evolved as people scaled one ridge after another and settled in the valleys between them. The pace of development and the places of early settlement were determined by the mountains and their rivers. Much of the wealth of West Virginia is deep within its hills: coal, natural gas, petroleum, and stone. Above these buried but rich natural resources, forested peaks and wooded valleys provide food and shelter to people across the state.

The beauty of the mountains draws large numbers of visitors to West Virginia. They fish in the mountain streams, hunt in the tree-covered hills, and hike the scenic trails. In the winter they come to ski down the snowy slopes, and in the summer they come for whitewater rafting. Adventurous visitors climb up the sides of the mountains and go down into their caves. They explore the state's peaks and valleys on horseback, on bicycles, and in all-terrain vehicles (ATVs).

West Virginia has three state songs, all praising its most prominent feature: the rugged mountains with their beautiful hills. Is it any wonder that John Denver, writing his nostalgic song "Country Roads," described West Virginia as "almost heaven"?

Chapter 1

THE GEOGRAPHY OF WEST VIRGINIA

West Virginia is not very big. In fact, only nine states are smaller. It was carved out of what used to be the very large state of Virginia. It's also bordered by Kentucky, Ohio, Pennsylvania, and Maryland.

The Appalachians

West Virginia lies entirely within the Appalachian Mountain range. Although not nearly as tall as the mountains of the western United States, the Appalachians are the highest mountains east of the Mississippi River. The Appalachians are actually a series of mountain ranges that parallel the Atlantic coastline from northeast Canada almost to the Gulf of Mexico. The Appalachian ranges in West Virginia are the Blue Ridge and the Alleghenies.

The eastern sixth of the state lies in the portion of the mountains called the Appalachian Ridge and Valley Province. It's called "ridge and valley" because it consists of rows, or ridges, of peaks separated by valleys. To the west of the Ridge and Valley Province, the bulk of the state is part of the Appalachian Plateau, also called the Allegheny Plateau. Here, the mountains are a little lower, more rounded, and not quite as rugged. The Allegheny Front separates the two regions. The front is a series of steep cliffs where the elevation changes sharply. The peaks to the east of the front are 3,000 to 4,000 feet (900 to 1,200 meters) high. The hills to the west of the front average 1,000 feet (300 m).

Six Regions

West Virginia's hills and rivers divide the state into six distinct sections—three in the narrow Ridge and Valley Province and three in the Allegheny Plateau.

The northern part of the eastern sixth of West Virginia is the Potomac Highlands. This area has the tallest mountains in the state. The South Branch of the Potomac River has cut a deep valley through the region. The area has dense forests, impressive rock formations, labyrinths of caves, and streams

A hiker stands atop a sandstone outcropping in Bear Rocks Preserve in the Alleghenies. On a clear day, hikers can see seven mountain ridges.

teeming with trout. Much of the area is protected forest and wilderness, including the 910,155-acre (368,326 hectares) Monongahela National Forest.

At the northeastern tip of the Potomac Highlands, the Eastern Panhandle juts to the southeast. The eastern edge of this region is part of the Great Valley of the Shenandoah River. It's lower in elevation than other parts of the state, and its gently rolling hills and fertile soil make it perfect for farms and small communities.

The Land

At one time, trees covered the mountains of West Virginia. Herds of bison thundered over the hills. Elk, puma, gray wolves, and deer roamed freely and widely. Wild turkeys, fishers, and eagles were plentiful. Beavers and river otters were abundant in the rivers and streams. This land was the hunting grounds of several Native American tribes.

By 1700, Europeans had begun moving into what is now West Virginia. The early settlers cut down many of the territory's trees to build houses and forts and to heat their homes. Later residents cleared large areas for towns and cities and to create grazing land for cattle. From the 1800s to the 1920s, an aggressive timber industry harvested lumber from large portions of the remaining forests. Even more trees were cut down to make room for railroad tracks and to provide ties for railroads.

As their habitat was gradually destroyed, the state's wildlife began disappearing. At the same time, hunters sought West Virginia's big game for meat and fur. By 1890, all of the elk were gone. In 1825, the last bison was killed. And by 1900, no gray wolves remained. Even the beaver, otter, and fisher populations were completely eradicated (destroyed).

In the 1930s, some conservationists began to reintroduce beavers to the state's rivers. Later, fishers and river otters were also brought back. Today, trees and shrubs have been planted and new forests are growing where tall ones once stood. Animals are protected in special wildlife areas and state and national parks and forests. The bison, elk, and gray wolves are gone, but the numbers of black bears, deer, and other animals native to West Virginia are again growing.

The southern end of the Ridge and Valley Province is the New River/Greenbrier Valley section. Here, the whitewater of the New and Greenbrier rivers has carved magnificent gorges and spectacular limestone caverns. Other waters bubble up from the ground in both sulfur springs and sweet springs. With its rushing rivers, walls of rock, miles of trails, and scenic beauty, it is an outdoor lover's paradise. This area is also rich in coal.

On the Allegheny Plateau, the northern section includes the Northern Panhandle that juts between Ohio and Pennsylvania. Among the mountains of the north are industrial plants, universities, and large cities.

The western border of the state is the Ohio River. Along its shores, the land is low and the soil good. A number of cities, mostly small, line the Ohio Valley region, and farms spread across the lowlands and the gentle hills.

The last of the six regions is the central section in the middle of the state. It is sometimes called the Mountain Lakes region. West Virginia has no natural lakes, but dams on the many rivers of this area have created five large lakes. People come here for fishing, sailing, water skiing, windsurfing, scuba diving, and whitewater rafting.

Climate

In the Appalachians, elevation instead of location has the biggest effect on the climate. The small state of West Virginia has three different life zones. These are areas with distinct climate, vegetation, and animal life.

The highest spots, in the Ridge and Valley Province, are in the Canadian Zone. As in Canada, summers are cool and winters are cold, with up to 200 inches (500 centimeters) of snow. The lowest

Glade Creek Mill, in Babcock State Park in southeastern West Virginia, was rebuilt from parts of three mills that were in the area around 1890. It is fully operational.

spots, along the Ohio River and in the Eastern Panhandle, are in the Carolinian Zone. As in North and South Carolina, summers are hot and winters are mild. About half of the state—the higher elevations of the Appalachian Plateau and the lower elevations of the Ridge and Valley Province—is between the two, in the Alleghenian Zone. This is a transition zone between Canadian and Carolinian climates, with summers that are warm but not hot, and winters that are cold but not harsh.

Plants

West Virginia's three life zones support a variety of vegetation. Three quarters of the state is forested with seventy-five different species of trees. High in the eastern mountains, in the Canadian Zone, the forests are softwood, or evergreen. They include pine, hemlock, and different kinds of spruce. In lowland areas, hardwoods, or deciduous trees, abound, with leaves that turn brilliant colors in autumn. These include oak, maple, birch, red ash, hickory, and poplar. Fruit and nut trees grace farms and orchards, including apple, black cherry, plum, pawpaw, walnut, chestnut, hickory, beech, and hazelnut trees. Both hardwoods and softwoods grow in the transition zone.

More than two hundred flowering trees and shrubs can be found throughout the state, including laurel, dogwood, redbud, and pussy willow. In some places, rhododendron, the state flower, grows in dense thickets beneath red spruce trees. Wild blackberries, cranberries, huckleberries, and raspberries thrive in clearings.

Animals

West Virginia's lush vegetation provides food and shelter for more than seventy types of wild animals. Black bear live in the pine forests, and deer can be seen throughout the state. Wildcats and foxes roam the woodlands. Hares are common in the high forests, and cottontails make their homes in the valleys. Squirrels are plentiful in the hardwood forests, and the state has opossums, raccoons, chipmunks, woodchucks, skunks, and fishers (weasel-like animals). The rivers and streams are home to beavers and otters, and several types of bats live in the underground caves. One animal peculiar to the high forests of the area is the West Virginia northern flying squirrel. The small animal spreads its four legs, its loose skin forming a parachute, and appears to fly as it glides from tree to tree.

Of the sixty species of amphibians and reptiles found in West Virginia, the most common are frogs, turtles, salamanders, lizards, and skinks. Hikers and boaters may encounter several types of nonpoisonous snakes, as well as copperheads and timber rattlesnakes. Twenty percent of the state's 178 species of fish are game fish—the kind that draw sportsmen to the rivers and lakes. These include bass, trout, pike, bluegill, and catfish.

The West Virginia Raptor Rehabilitation Center cares for injured and orphaned birds of prey. This high school student is working with an American bald eagle named Thunder.

More than three hundred species of birds live in West Virginia for at least part of the year. Many types of small birds fill the air with song and color. Bird watchers can spot whippoorwills, cardinals (the state bird), tanagers, bobolinks, woodpeckers, orioles, finches, mockingbirds, bluebirds, robins, thrushes, wrens, nuthatches, and sparrows. Waterfowl come to the rivers and lakes during migration season: grebes, loons, ducks, geese, herons, and bitterns. Others are found along stream banks: plovers, quails, woodcocks, snipes, and sandpipers. Large predatory birds soar over the forest trees: great horned owls, hawks, turkey vultures, bald eagles, and golden eagles.

Chapter 2

THE HISTORY OF
WEST VIRGINIA

Before Europeans came to America, an ancient people wandered in the Ohio and Kanawha river valleys. They were hunter-gatherers, living off the fruits and animals of the land. Little is known of these early people except that they built mounds over the remains of their dead. So historians call them Mound Builders. The cone-shaped mounds they left behind are massive structures, with one grave built atop another. The largest is 69 feet (21 m) high. The Mound Builders were long gone by the time the first Europeans came.

Exploration and Settlement

For more than sixty years after settlers from England established the Virginia Colony in 1607, no one ventured across the Appalachians. In 1669, Virginia's Governor William Berkeley sent John Lederer to explore what lay beyond the mountains. In his three expeditions, Lederer was probably the first white man to scale the Blue Ridge and see the Shenandoah Valley. In 1671, Thomas Batts and Robert Fallam crossed the Appalachians to the New River and claimed the land for England.

Before long, fur traders were moving into the area, and the French were exploring as well. The governor of the Virginia Colony wanted

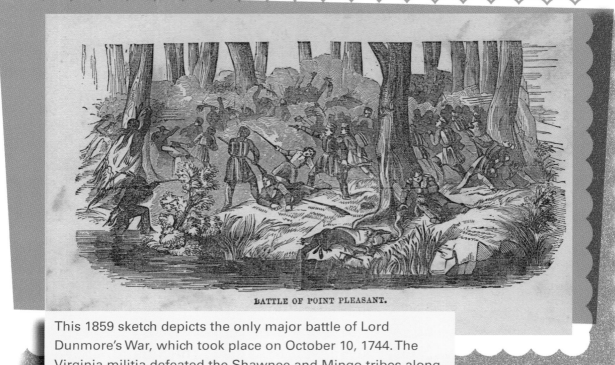

BATTLE OF POINT PLEASANT.

This 1859 sketch depicts the only major battle of Lord Dunmore's War, which took place on October 10, 1744. The Virginia militia defeated the Shawnee and Mingo tribes along the Ohio River.

to keep the French from advancing toward his colony. So he encouraged people to cross the Blue Ridge and settle in the part of the colony that was becoming known as western Virginia. He gave land to people who would settle families there.

When the first settlers moved down the South Branch of the Potomac into the Shenandoah Valley, they encountered no villages and no people who had a previous legal and formal claim to the land. But the area was part of the traditional hunting grounds of Native Americans.

Conflicts with Native Americans

The early relationships between English colonists and Native Americans in western Virginia were friendly. The colonists received furs from the Indians, which they sold in England, and the Indians received guns, steel hatchets, cloth, and other goods. The trade was mutually beneficial. But settlers soon began cutting trees, clearing large patches of land, killing animals, and bringing cows to graze on land that belonged to elk and deer. Native Americans saw their way of life threatened. As more and more white settlers moved onto their hunting grounds, the Native Americans attacked the settlements in an attempt to chase the Europeans off.

Periods of peace were interrupted by sporadic attacks and wars between English colonists and Native Americans. Conflict continued until 1794. In that year, General "Mad" Anthony Wayne won an important military victory, and the tribes retreated west of the Ohio River.

A New State

As western Virginia grew in population and prosperity, it became increasingly different from the eastern portion of the state. Western Virginia was mainly made up of small, family-operated farms, while eastern Virginia consisted of large plantations dependent on slave labor. Industry had begun in the west, spurred by the discovery of coal and natural gas. Agriculture remained the occupation of the east. Westerners were hard-working, rough-edged pioneers. Easterners thought of themselves as more sophisticated, refined, and cultured.

The increasing cultural and economic differences led to conflicts between the two parts of the state. Eastern and western Virginians

Harpers Ferry

Sometime in the mid-1700s, a Pennsylvanian named Robert Harper decided to make his home where the Potomac and Shenandoah rivers meet. Settlers were coming down the Shenandoah, and Harper saw a business opportunity. In 1761, he began operating a ferry across the Potomac. The little enterprise grew into a bustling community, and people called the place Harpers Ferry.

President George Washington built an arsenal and armory at Harpers Ferry. The arsenal attracted other industries, and the town grew. When a canal and railroad reached the town, Harpers Ferry, now on the main thoroughfare between the nation's capital and points south, grew even larger.

It was the arsenal that brought fame to Harpers Ferry. John Brown had long eyed the guns there. He was an abolitionist—a person who wanted to abolish, or do away with, slavery. In 1859, Brown and a small group of men stormed the arsenal and seized the weapons. His plan was to lead a slave rebellion and free all the slaves. But the army retook the arsenal and put an end to Brown's plan.

Two years later, the Civil War was on, and Harpers Ferry was an important battleground of that war. The city changed hands at least eight times. Both the Union and the Confederacy wanted not only the arsenal, but also control of the canal and the railroad. The fighting completely destroyed the city.

Attempts to rebuild the town after the Civil War achieved little. For a brief period in the 1900s, Harpers Ferry was a resort town. But after hard economic times and floods, it again became a ghost town. In 1944, the National Park Service turned most of the town into a historical park. Today, about three hundred people live in Harpers Ferry. It is the most frequently visited spot in the state, drawing two million tourists every year.

argued over representation in the state government, taxes, and slavery. Just before the Civil War began in 1861, Virginia seceded from the Union, joining the rebellious Confederacy. Representatives from several of the counties of western Virginia met in the city of Wheeling to determine what to do as the country raced toward war. Some were for the Union and some for the Confederacy. Some wanted

When Virginia seceded in 1861, U.S. soldiers burned the arsenal at Harpers Ferry to keep it out of Confederate hands. Citizens saved some of the weapons and moved them to Richmond.

to declare the government of Virginia not legitimate and reorganize the state. Others wanted to separate from Virginia and form their own state. Divisions were very deep, but eventually those who favored separation from Virginia won.

Representatives from western Virginia wrote a constitution and asked to be admitted to the Union as a state. At first, President Abraham Lincoln questioned whether sixty-three counties could legally secede from a state. In the end, Lincoln accepted the request. On June 20, 1863, West Virginia became the thirty-fifth state.

Industrialization

After the Civil War, the nation's attention turned to rebuilding. West Virginia had already begun a shift from an agricultural economy to an industrial one. Massive deposits of salt, coal, natural gas, and oil

Two teenage boys work in a West Virginia coal mine in 1908. Coal oil lamps on their caps provided lighting, and animals carried the coal out of the mine.

had been found, and industries had sprung up around them. After the war, there was great demand for the iron, steel, and glass that West Virginia factories could produce. There was even greater demand for its coal and timber. The railroads made it easy to get these products to other parts of the country. West Virginia's coal fed the factories of America's Industrial Revolution.

Coal mining became the state's primary occupation. Other industries also became established, but nearly all of them depended on coal to power their operations. The jobs available in the mines drew new people to the state—African Americans newly liberated from the fields and immigrants from many European countries. Tiny farming towns became booming urban centers almost overnight. Because the railroads carried West Virginia's coal to the Northeast and the Midwest, money poured into the state. The coal boom lasted until the Great Depression of the 1930s.

West Virginia Today

Coal mining remains the mainstay of West Virginia's economy. The state's fortunes have risen and fallen according to the country's demand for coal. After World War II, people began to use more oil and electricity and less coal. Mine owners could not sell as much coal, and many miners lost their jobs. At that time, West Virginia had the highest unemployment rate in the nation. In the 1970s, energy demand grew at the same time that oil-producing Middle Eastern countries refused to ship oil to the United States. So the price of coal climbed as Americans sought alternative energy sources to gas and oil. In the 1980s, however, energy prices fell again and new mining techniques opened up coal reserves in the western states. As a result, West Virginia's economy suffered again.

Heavy reliance on a single industry has created problems for the people of West Virginia. The state, in the heart of Appalachia, has become known for high poverty. However, West Virginia has begun to develop and attract new industries, particularly tourism. The hills that gave it great mineral resources are continuing to yield wealth in the form of thousands of visitors and outdoor enthusiasts every year.

Chapter 3

THE GOVERNMENT OF WEST VIRGINIA

As with the other states of the Union, the governing system of West Virginia is much like that of the federal government of the United States. It is a representative government with three distinct branches: legislative, executive, and judicial. Each branch has certain responsibilities and specific powers. That way, no one branch becomes more powerful than another.

Legislative Branch

The legislative branch is responsible for making laws. The West Virginia Legislature is very similar to the U.S. Congress. It is made up of two bodies: the senate and the house of delegates.

The state is divided into seventeen senatorial districts. Each district is supposed to have about the same number of citizens. Each district elects two senators, making a total of thirty-four senators. Each serves a four-year term, and elections are held every two years. In each district, the two senators are elected in alternating election years. That means half of the senate seats are being voted on in every election, and half of the senators are always veterans with at least two years of experience.

To elect members to the house of delegates, the state is divided into fifty-eight house districts. The population is not evenly divided among these districts, so thirty-five of the districts have one delegate each and the others have from two to seven each. The total number of delegates is one hundred. Delegates serve two-year terms.

West Virginia's legislature is called a citizen legislature because serving as a senator or a delegate is not a full-time job. The legislature meets only once a year and for no more than sixty days.

Because it's a small state in terms of population, West Virginia has only three representatives in the U.S. Congress. The three representatives, along with the state's two senators, give it five electoral votes when it is time to elect the president of the country.

The State Capitol Building in Charleston is the tallest building in West Virginia at 292 feet (89 m).

Executive Branch

The executive branch is responsible for carrying out the laws enacted by the West Virginia Legislature and for running the day-to-day

The State Capital

When western Virginians first discussed forming their own state, they met in Wheeling, a city in the Northern Panhandle. When they wrote the constitution for the new state, they again met in Wheeling. So when President Abraham Lincoln proclaimed the new state of West Virginia in 1863, the logical place for the state's capital was Wheeling.

By 1870, people were serving in the state legislature who had not participated in making the original decisions regarding the state constitution and government several years earlier. Some were not happy with the government offices being located in the far northern section of the state, and they voted to move the capital out of Wheeling. Citizens of Kanawha County sent a steamboat up the Ohio River, loaded all the state records on it, and brought them down the Ohio and up the Kanawha to the new capital of Charleston.

Not everyone was pleased with this new arrangement, however. In 1875, the legislature voted again, this time to move the capital back to Wheeling. Again, the government records were brought by steamship, this time up the Ohio from Charleston to Wheeling. But the state offices were not to remain there for long either. In 1877, the legislature decided to settle the matter by a vote of the people. Given the choice of Charleston, Clarksburg, or Martinsburg, West Virginians chose Charleston as the permanent site for the state capital. In 1885, boats once more carried their cargo of state documents south.

But the competition for the seat of government did not end in Charleston. In 1921, the capitol building burned to the ground, and people in Clarksburg, Parkersburg, and Huntington asked to relocate the government offices to their cities. Instead, a new capitol was built—which also was destroyed by fire six years later. Today, after a decade-long, $10 million restoration in the 1920s, a beautiful capitol building again stands in Charleston. It appears the offices of the state government have found a permanent home and will remain in Charleston for good.

business of the state. Six executive officials are elected: governor, secretary of state, auditor, treasurer, commissioner of agriculture, and attorney general. The governor is the chief executive officer. The governor serves a four-year term and may be reelected to a second term. If a governor serves eight years, he or she may be elected again after a different governor serves at least one term.

The Executive Mansion in Charleston is where the governor and his or her family live. Built in 1926, it overlooks the Kanawha River and contains thirty rooms.

Judicial Branch

The judicial branch has the responsibility of interpreting West Virginia's laws and making sure they are carried out fairly. Judges hear complaints, settle legal disputes, decide if people are guilty or innocent of crimes, protect citizens' rights, and punish people who break the law. West Virginia has five levels of courts: family, municipal (city), magistrate (local), circuit (one or more counties), and supreme. All judges are elected, not appointed. Circuit court judges serve eight-year terms, and supreme court judges serve twelve-year terms. Judges of the lower-level courts do not have to be lawyers, but circuit court judges have to practice law for five years before becoming judges. Supreme court judges must have ten years of experience practicing law.

Cass Gilbert designed West Virginia's supreme court chamber without a traditional bar before the bench to symbolize that nothing separates the court from the citizens it serves. Gilbert later modeled the U.S. Supreme Court chambers after West Virginia's.

The highest court, the supreme court of appeals, is the only appellate court in the state. That means any time someone disagrees with a circuit court ruling and appeals to a higher court, the matter goes straight to the supreme court of appeals. In addition to hearing appeals, this court decides if state laws are constitutional, and it rules on the actions of state officials. The court is required to meet twice a year, in January and September, and it may hold special sessions when necessary.

Chapter 4

THE ECONOMY OF WEST VIRGINIA

West Virginia's wealth has always been in its mountains. The fertile land along the rivers of its mountain valleys sustained an early farming economy. After the Civil War, the mountain forests and the resources underground fed an industrial boom. During World War I, manufacturing was added to the economy as the state began to produce large quantities of glass, chemicals, steel, and textiles. As the strength of the coal industry rose and fell, recreation and tourism—made possible by beautiful mountain settings—became major sectors of the economy, beginning in the 1990s. Today, all of these industries continue to contribute to the economy of the Mountain State.

Agriculture

The agricultural sector of a state's economy includes money earned from the cultivation of plants and the raising of animals. In West Virginia, 82 percent of agriculture comes from animals, or livestock, and livestock products. Of all agricultural products, plant and animal, the biggest sellers are broilers—young chickens. Beef cattle are the next most important commodity, followed by eggs, dairy products, and turkeys. The state also produces hogs, sheep (for both meat and wool), honey, and farm-raised fish.

Farms in West Virginia such as this one are often nestled against the rolling hills of the lower elevations.

The state's number-one crop is hay, grown primarily to feed livestock. However, several other crops are also good sources of revenue. Although small, West Virginia ranks eighth in the country in production of apples and thirteenth in peaches. Other agricultural products include wheat, corn, soybeans, and tobacco. Most of the agricultural activity takes place around the streams of the Potomac highlands and in the Ohio and Kanawha river valleys.

Natural Resources

Coal is still king in West Virginia. It's mined in twenty-six of the state's fifty-five counties. West Virginia is second in the nation in coal production, yielding 161 million tons (164 tonnes) in 2007. But its hills also have other natural resources: natural gas, petroleum, stone, salt, sand, and gravel.

These underground resources form the basis of a strong manufacturing sector. Metals such as steel and aluminum are produced in the mills of West Virginia. The state's factories produce chemicals, cement, synthetics, machinery, glass, and pottery. Most of the manufacturing is located in the industrial areas of the Northern Panhandle and the Ohio and Kanawha river valleys.

A barge loaded with coal travels on the Kanawha River. About 7 percent of the coal mined in the United States comes from the Kanawha River Valley in West Virginia.

Forests

Even with 21,400 farms and several large cities, two-thirds of West Virginia, or 12 million acres (5 million ha), consist of forests. The forest products industry employs about thirty thousand people. The cutting of trees in the hardwood forests is carefully managed so that, unlike in times past, timber will always be available. The rate of tree growth is now faster than the rate of harvesting.

In addition to timber, West Virginia's forests produce fruits and nuts, as well as medicinal plants. Some trees in the state's pine forests are harvested for Christmas trees.

Coal Mining

Although coal was first discovered in West Virginia in 1742, it lay untapped for nearly a century. At first, the coal was surface-mined with picks and shovels. That is, men used picks to break up the ground to get to the coal that lay fairly close to the surface. They then shoveled the coal into sacks. As demand grew and prices rose, workers tunneled into mines and used mules, goats, or oxen to carry out the buried store of coal.

In the 1890s, machinery was introduced into mining operations: machines that cut coal out of the ground, machines that loaded it into containers, and tractors that hauled it out of the mines. Larger and more efficient machinery was developed. Eventually, the machines allowed one coal miner to do the work that was once done by four to seven men using picks and shovels.

Some of the earliest methods of mining were very dangerous. In bell-pit mines (vertical shafts that opened into a chamber, somewhat resembling a bell shape), coal was cut out until the narrow sides began to cave in. In room-and-pillar mines, a series of underground "rooms" were dug, and pillars of coal were left standing to support the roof. This method is still in use today.

Modern methods of coal mining offer greater safety. Many of the 550 mines in West Virginia use mountaintop removal mining. Instead of tunneling into the mountain to get to the coal, the top of the mountain is blasted away. The coal is then extracted through surface mining techniques, and the displaced rocks and dirt are used to fill in previously mined areas and dry river beds. Thus, when the coal has been removed, the mines are "reclaimed." The filled-in dirt is leveled, and real estate developers can build on the site. Golf courses, shopping centers, airports, and schools are now located where coal was once mined.

Recreation and Tourism

West Virginia's forests make possible one of the state's most successful industries: outdoor adventure. Every year, thousands of people visit the many natural attractions of the Mountain State. The West Virginia Division of Tourism has reported that travel spending by out-of-state guests totals nearly $4 billion annually. People come to ski in the winter and water ski in the summer. They visit West Virginia to go boating and white-water rafting, hike the scenic routes, explore the caves, watch the birds, and visit historic landmarks. And they come to hunt and fish.

Cross-country skiers in the Dolly Sods Wilderness, located in eastern West Virginia, maneuver around impressive rock formations and stands of red spruce.

Hunting and fishing are major contributors to the state's economy. Licenses alone bring in almost $16,000 annually. And when people hunt and fish, they also spend money on local food, lodging, transportation, and supplies. The recreation and tourism industry, together with their related activities, is the fastest-growing sector of West Virginia's economy.

Chapter 5

PEOPLE FROM WEST VIRGINIA:
PAST AND PRESENT

The Mountain State has produced many famous and accomplished military members, athletes, entertainers, authors, scientists, and mathematicians. Following are just a few of West Virginia's proud sons and daughters.

Pearl S. Buck (1892–1973) One of the most famous daughters of West Virginia, Pearl Buck (born in Hillsboro) spent very little of her life in the state. Born to missionary parents, she lived her first forty years in China, with brief trips home to the United States. While teaching at Nanking University, she began writing. Her second novel, the Pulitzer Prize–winning *The Good Earth*, was the best-selling book of 1931 and 1932. Buck wrote more than seventy books and was the first American woman to be awarded the Nobel Prize in Literature. She founded Welcome House, an international interracial adoption agency, and the Pearl S. Buck Foundation, which has helped thousands of children in many Asian countries.

Sam Huff (1934–) At age twenty-four, Sam Huff (born in Edna Gas) went from a coal camp to the cover of *Time*

Pearl S. Buck is shown at home in 1965. Long before computers were invented, Buck composed more than eighty novels and other literary works on a typewriter.

magazine. His salvation from the mines was football. A star in high school, Huff was recruited by West Virginia University, and from there by the New York Giants. His big break came when the Giants' starting middle linebacker was injured. Huff was sent into the game as a substitute. In thirteen seasons—eight with the Giants and five with the Washington Redskins—he played in six NFL Championship games and five Pro Bowls. In 1982, Huff was inducted into the Pro Football Hall of Fame.

General Thomas "Stonewall" Jackson (1824–1863) U.S. Army officer Thomas Jackson (born in Clarksburg) was a professor when the Civil War broke out. He returned to active service, this time in the Confederate Army of Virginia. At the First Battle of Bull Run, Jackson earned the nickname "Stonewall," probably because of his toughness and determination. After a win at the Battle of Chancellorsville, Jackson was mistakenly wounded by his own soldiers guarding their camp. He had to have an arm amputated. General Robert E. Lee, leader of the Confederate forces, said of his trusted aide Jackson, "He has lost his left arm, but I have lost my right arm." Eight days after the incident, Jackson died after contracting pneumonia.

Don Knotts (1924–2006) In high school, Don Knotts (born in Morgantown) developed a comedy and ventriloquist act and performed at school and in churches. In the army during World War II, he served as an entertainer in a variety show called "Stars and Gripes." He developed the fidgety, bumbling character that would make him famous early in his career as

The Hatfields and McCoys

The longstanding war between the Hatfields and the McCoys really was a true family feud. Randolph (Ran'l) McCoy and his fifteen children lived on the Kentucky side of the Tug Fork River. Anderson (Devil Anse) Hatfield and his thirteen children lived on the West Virginia side of the river. As was common in the sparsely populated mountains, more than one Hatfield had married a McCoy over the years. Despite intermarrying, the two families bickered repeatedly, and these spats often turned violent.

The first big fight occurred in 1878. Ran'l McCoy accused Floyd Hatfield, his wife's brother-in-law, of stealing one of his pigs, a serious offense in those days. A jury of six McCoys and six Hatfields acquitted Floyd, but the McCoys remained angry. One of them killed the star witness for Floyd, who happened to be related to both families.

A budding romance between one of Ran'l's daughters and one of Devil Anse's sons triggered the next major incident in 1882. Three of Ran'l's sons killed one of Devil Anse's brothers. Three days later, the three McCoys were also dead. More tits-for-tats followed, and by 1891, the feud had claimed thirteen lives.

A little more than a hundred years after the violence ended, a great-great-great-grandson of Ran'l McCoy organized a reunion of the two families. He hoped members of the families would get to know one another and the event would draw tourist dollars to the section of Appalachia where the feud once raged. Five thousand people attended the first reunion in 2000. Today, the Hatfield-McCoy Reunion has become an annual event that includes a tug of war across the Tug River. Hatfields and McCoys may struggle against each other and wage "war" across the river, but now it is all in the name of fun.

a regular on *The Steve Allen Show*. Of his many movie, television, and cartoon voice-over roles, Knotts is best known as Deputy Barney Fife on *The Andy Griffith Show*. He earned five Emmy awards for the role.

Kathy Mattea (1959–) Before she cut the album *Coal* in 2008, Kathy Mattea (born in South Charleston) had already won two Grammys and several other music awards. But coal was in her blood. Both of her grandfathers were miners who raised their children in coal camps. Her mother worked for the miners' union. Remembering the Farmington mine disaster in 1968 and the catastrophe in the Sago mine in 2006, Mattea put together a collection of coal mining songs. As a proud West Virginian, she selected music that would permit her to be "a voice for a whole group of people, a place, [and] a way of life" (as quoted on Mattea's official Web site).

Jon Andrew McBride (1943–) After graduating from West Virginia University, Jon McBride (born in Charleston) joined the U.S. Navy at the beginning of the Vietnam War. As a Navy fighter pilot, he flew sixty-four combat missions. After the war, McBride became a test pilot, logging more than 8,800 hours testing 40 types of military and civilian planes. He then became an astronaut. In 1984, McBride piloted the seven-man *Challenger* space orbiter during an eight-day mission in space.

John Forbes Nash Jr. (1928–) When he was just a child, the parents of John Nash (born in Bluefield) recognized his genius. He took college classes in his hometown while he was still in high school and earned a master's degree in three years. He received a Ph.D. from Princeton, where he later taught. A brilliant mathematician, Nash struggled for thirty years with paranoid schizophrenia and was in and out of mental hospitals. He received a Nobel Prize in Economics in 1994 for work he began in 1950. His story was told in the book *A Beautiful Mind* (1998), which was the basis for a somewhat fictionalized 2002 movie of the same name.

John Forbes Nash Jr. stands in front of the mathematics building on the campus of Princeton University.

John C. Norman (1930–)

Born in Charleston, John Norman became a cardiovascular (heart) surgeon. In addition to practicing surgery, he taught at Harvard and performed medical research. He was part of a team pioneering research on organ transplants, and his work helped make transplants of hearts and other organs possible. After working in several cities throughout the country, he returned to West Virginia in 1986 as chairman of the surgery department of the Marshall University School of Medicine.

Mary Lou Retton (1968–)

At the age of sixteen, Mary Lou Retton (born in Fairmont) became suddenly famous.

Perfectly poised on the balance beam, Mary Lou Retton delivers a stunning performance at the 1984 Summer Olympic Games in Los Angeles.

A gymnast with seven championship titles, she won five medals in the 1984 Summer Olympics, the most anyone received at the games that year. Her gold medal in the Women's All-Around was the first won by an American woman in any Olympic gymnastic event. That year, *Sports Illustrated* named Retton "Sportswoman of the Year." Not only her talent, but also her smile and her attitude captured hearts. In 1993, she was voted the "Most Popular Athlete in America" in a survey conducted by Nye Lavalle's Sports Marketing Group. Retired from gymnastics, Retton is now a public speaker, a sports commentator, and an actress.

Chuck Yeager (1923–) When Chuck Yeager (born in Myra) enlisted in the U.S. Army Air Forces (a precursor to the U.S. Air Force), he wanted only to be an airplane mechanic. But when World War II broke out, pilots were needed. Yeager became a fighter pilot, flying sixty-four missions and shooting down at least eleven enemy planes. After the war, he worked as an Air Force test pilot, testing new aircraft. At age twenty-four, Yeager was the first person to break the sound barrier, flying faster than the speed of sound. He had a long and distinguished military career, one of the very few people to go from enlisted man to Air Force general.

Timeline

1500 BCE–1000 CE	Mound builders and other Native Americans live in the Ohio and Kanawha river valleys.
1669–1670	John Lederer makes three expeditions into western Virginia, becoming the first European to see the land that would become known as West Virginia.
1671	Thomas Batts and Robert Fallam reach the New River and claim the area for England.
1730	Settlers begin moving into western Virginia Colony.
1742	John Howard and John Peter Salley discover coal near present-day Racine on the Coal River.
1771	John Floyd discovers natural gas in Kanawha Valley.
1794	"Mad" Anthony Wayne's victory at Fallen Timbers, Ohio, ends the Indian wars.
1859	John Brown attacks the U.S. arsenal at Harpers Ferry in an unsuccessful attempt to start a slave uprising. He is hanged in Charles Town.
1861	Representatives of several western Virginia counties meet several times in Wheeling, denounce Virginia's secession from the Union, and begin to create a new state and write a constitution.
1863	West Virginia is admitted to the Union as the thirty-fifth state.
1861–1865	About thirty-two thousand western Virginians fight for the Union and ten thousand fight for the Confederacy during the American Civil War.
1912–1921	Conflicts erupt between miners and mine owners over labor unions in what becomes known as the Coal Mine Wars.
1973–1974	The Middle Eastern oil embargo begins a major resurgence in the U.S. coal industry.
2008–2009	West Virginia loses twenty-three thousand jobs in a twelve-month period during a global recession. Job losses occur in many industries, including manufacturing, mining, construction, retail, and tourism.
2009	The federal government weighs a crackdown on mountaintop mining and power plant emissions, a move that would affect employment and income in West Virginia.

West Virginia at a Glance

State motto:	*Montani semper liberi* ("Mountaineers are always free")
State capital:	Charleston
State tree:	Sugar maple
State bird:	Cardinal
State flower:	Rhododendron
State fruit:	Golden Delicious apple
State fish:	Brook trout
Statehood date and number:	June 20, 1863; thirty-fifth state
State nickname:	The Mountain State
Total area and U.S. rank:	24,231 square miles (62,758 sq km); forty-first largest state
Population:	1,808,000
Highest elevation:	Spruce Knob, at 4,863 feet (1,482 m)
Lowest elevation:	Harpers Ferry, at 240 feet (73 m)
Major rivers:	Potomac River, Monongahela River, Cheat River, Ohio River, Guyandotte River, Greenbrier River, Kanawha River, Big Sandy River, Tug Fork River, New River, Capacon River

State flag

State seal

Major lakes:	Tygart Lake, Bluestone Lake, East Lynn Lake, Summersville Lake, Sutton Lake
Hottest recorded temperature:	112°F (44°C), at Martinsburg, July 10, 1935
Coldest recorded temperature:	-37°F (-38°C), at Lewisburg, December 30, 1917
Origin of state name:	West Virginia was formed from part of the western area of the state of Virginia; Virginia was named after Queen Elizabeth I, the "Virgin Queen"
Chief agricultural products:	Chickens, cattle, dairy products, turkeys, hay, apples, peaches, corn, eggs, hogs, sheep, oats, barley, wheat, tobacco, cherries, blackberries
Major industries:	Mining (coal), chemical manufacturing, glass products, tourism

Cardinal

Rhododendron

armory A facility for manufacturing guns and ammunition.

arsenal A facility for storing weapons and ammunition.

capital The city in which the government offices of a state or country are located.

Confederacy The Confederate States of America, the group of Southern states that seceded from the United States and fought the U.S. Army in the Civil War.

deciduous Refers to trees that lose their leaves in the fall.

eradicate To remove completely.

executive Refers to the branch of government responsible for carrying out laws and the day-to-day business of governing.

gorge A narrow passage between hills.

hardwoods Deciduous trees and the woods made from them.

judiciary Refers to the branch of government responsible for interpreting law, settling legal disputes, and punishing crimes.

legislature A governmental body responsible for making laws.

panhandle A bit of land, usually a narrow strip, connected to a larger land area, resembling the handle of a pan.

plateau A large stretch of high land that is fairly level.

rapids Portion of a stream or river where the water falls quickly down an incline.

ridge and valley Land type consisting of parallel ridges, or rows, of mountains separated by valleys.

secede To separate from.

softwoods Evergreen trees and the woods made from them.

white water Rapidly moving water that is frothy; also called rapids.

FOR MORE INFORMATION

West Virginia Division of Culture and History

The Culture Center

Capitol Complex

1900 Kanawha Boulevard East

Charleston, WV 25305-0300

(304) 558-0220

Web site: http://www.wvculture.org/index.aspx

This government agency preserves and promotes the arts and history of the state. It houses archives of documents and articles on many historical topics.

West Virginia Division of Natural Resources

Building 74

324 Fourth Avenue

South Charleston, WV 25303

(304) 558-2754

Web site: http://www.wvdnr.gov

This agency provides information about wildlife, vegetation, hunting, fishing, and state parks.

West Virginia Division of Tourism

90 MacCorkle Avenue SW

South Charleston, WV 25303

(304) 558-2200

Web site: http://www.wvtourism.com/spec.aspx?pgid = 173

Maps, state facts and trivia, and more can be found on the Web site.

West Virginia Geological and Economic Survey

Mont Chateau Research Center

1 Mont Chateau Road

Morgantown, WV 26508-8079

(304) 594-2331

Web site: http://www.wvgs.wvnet.edu/www/index.html

This survey's Web site features articles on the geology and topography of the state and of specific regions, articles on coal mining, and statistics on individual counties.

West Virginia Government

Capitol Complex

1900 Kanawha Boulevard East

Charleston, WV 25305-0300

Web site: http://www.wv.gov/Pages/default.aspx

On this Web site, there is information on the various regions of the state, national and state parks and recreation areas, government, and people and events in the state's history.

West Virginia Legislature's Office of Reference and Information

Room MB-27, Building 1

State Capitol Complex

Charleston, WV 25305

(304) 347-4836

Web site: http://www.legis.state.wv.us/Joint/Pubinfo/legisinfo.cfm

Created by the Joint Committee on Government and Finance in 1976, the Office of Reference and Information disseminates information on all facets of the legislative process in West Virginia.

West Virginia State Parks

324 4th Avenue South

Charleston, WV 25303

(304) 558-2764

Web site: http://www.wvstateparks.com

The West Virginia State Parks system promotes conservation by preserving and protecting natural areas of unique or exceptional scenic, scientific, cultural, archaeological, or historical significance. It also provides outdoor recreational opportunities for all.

Web Sites

Due to the changing nature of Internet links, Rosen Publishing has developed an online list of Web sites related to the subject of this book. This site is updated regularly. Please use this link to access the list:

http://www.rosenlinks.com/uspp/wvpp

FOR FURTHER READING

Brown, Jonatha. *West Virginia* (Portraits of the States). Strongsville, OH: Gareth Stevens Publishing, 2006.

Cribben, Patrick. *Uniquely West Virginia* (Heinemann State Studies). Chicago, IL: Heinemann-Raintree, 2005.

Hanel, Rachel. *West Virginia* (This Land Called America). Mankato, MN: Creative Education, 2009.

Haning, Leslie. *The Mountaineer's Journey Through West Virginia*. Chantilly, VA: Mascot Books, 2008.

Labella, Susan. *West Virginia* (Rookie Read-About Geography). New York, NY: Children's Press, 2006.

Laskas, Gretchen Moran. *Miner's Daughter*. New York, NY: Simon & Schuster, 2007.

Olhoff, Jim. *West Virginia* (The United States). Edina, MN: Checkerboard Books, 2009.

Rand, Jonathan. *Wicked Velociraptors of West Virginia* (American Chillers). Indian River, MI: Audio Craft Press, 2008.

Shogan, Robert. *The Battle of Blair Mountain: The Story of America's Largest Labor Uprising*. New York, NY: Basic Books, 2006.

Slayton, Fran. *When the Whistle Blows*. New York, NY: Penguin Group, 2009.

Somervill, Barbara A. *West Virginia* (From Sea to Shining Sea). New York, NY: Children's Press, 2008.

Wyatt, Melissa. *Funny How Things Change*. New York, NY: Farrar, Straus and Giroux, 2009.

BIBLIOGRAPHY

About.com. "The Reunion They Said Would Never Happen." 2000. Retrieved September 2009 (http://genealogy.about.com/library/weekly/aa043000a.htm).

Conn, Peter. "Pearl S. Buck." University of Pennsylvania, 1996. Retrieved September 2009 (http://www.english.upenn.edu/Projects/Buck/biography.html).

De Hass, Willis. *History of the Early Settlement and Indian Wars of West Virginia.* Parsons, WV: McClain Printing Company, 1851.

Federal Writers Project. *West Virginia: A Guide to the Mountain State.* New York, NY: Oxford University Press, 1941.

Frenz, Horst, ed. "Pearl S. Buck." *Nobel Lectures, Literature 1901–1967.* Amsterdam, Netherlands: Elsevier Publishing Company, 1969.

Lewis, Virgil Anson. *History of West Virginia in Two Parts.* Philadelphia, PA: Hubbard Brothers, 1889.

Lugar, Norma. "Hatfield-McCoy Feud: Roseanna: Juliet of the Mountains." Blue Ridge Country, February 17, 2009. Retrieved September 2009 (http://www.blueridgecountry. com/archive/hatfields-and-mccoys.html).

MaryLouRetton.com. "Mary Lou Retton." Retrieved September 2009 (http://marylou retton.com/ml_biography.html).

Mattea.com. "Kathy Mattea." 2009. Retrieved September 2009 (http://www.mattea.com/ KathyMatteaHome2008.html).

National Aeronautics and Space Administration. "Biographical Data: John A. McBride." 2008. Retrieved September 2009 (http://www.jsc.nasa.gov/Bios/htmlbios/mcbride-ja.html).

NNDB.com. "Don Knotts." Retrieved September 2009 (http://www.nndb.com/ people/750/000022684).

Onkst, David H. "Chuck Yeager." U.S. Centennial of Flight Commission. Retrieved September 2009 (http://www.centennialofflight.gov/essay/Explorers_Record_ Setters_and_Daredevils/yeager/EX30.htm).

Pro Football Hall of Fame. "Sam Huff." Retrieved September 2009 (http://www.profoot ballhof.com/hof/member.aspx?PLAYER_ID=102).

Rice, Otis K., and Stephen W. Brown. *West Virginia: A History.* Lexington, KY: University Press of Kentucky, 1993.

Riddel, Frank S. *Historical Atlas of West Virginia.* Morgantown, WV: West Virginia University Press, 2008.

Savage, Lon. *Thunder in the Mountains: The West Virginia Mine War, 1920-21*. Pittsburgh, PA: University of Pittsburgh Press, 1990.

Sullivan, Ken, ed. *The West Virginia Encyclopedia*. Charleston, WV: West Virginia Humanities Council, 2006.

West Virginia Archives and History. "Native American Clashes with European Settlers." Retrieved September 2009 (http://www.wvculture.org/History/indland.html#settle).

West Virginia Archives and History. "West Virginia's Mine Wars." Retrieved September 2009 (http://www.wvculture.org/history/minewars.html).

West Virginia Division of Natural Resources. "Home Page." Retrieved August/September 2009 (http://www.wvdnr.gov).

West Virginia Facts. "Floating Capitol." 2005. Retrieved September 2009 (http://www.wvtourism.com/spec.aspx?pgid=80#FLOATING CAPITOL).

West Virginia Web. "Harpers Ferry." Retrieved September 2009 (http://www.wvweb.com/cities/harpers_ferry/index.html).

Williams, John Alexander. *West Virginia: A History*. Morgantown, WV: West Virginia University Press, 2003.

About the Author

A native of Virginia, Ann Byers is very familiar with the neighboring state of West Virginia. She knows the beauty and tragedy of life in Appalachia, as her grandfather died in a coal mining accident. Byers, her husband, and four grown children and their families now live in California.

Photo Credits

Cover (top left), p. 17 Library of Congress Prints and Photographs Division; cover (top right), pp. 7, 27 Raymond Gehman/National Geographic/Getty Images; cover (bottom) © www.istockphoto.com/John Brueske; pp. 3, 6, 13, 20, 25, 30, 38 National Park Service; p. 4 © GeoAtlas; p. 10 © www.istockphoto.com/Joanna Pecha; pp. 12, 18, 24 © AP Images; p. 14 The New York Public Library/Art Resource, NY; p. 21 © www.istockphoto.com/Henryk Sadura; p. 23 © James Lemass/SuperStock; p. 26 © www.istockphoto.com/david olah; p. 29 Skip Brown/National Geographic/Getty Images; p. 31 Reginald Davis/Time & Life Pictures/Getty Images; p. 35 Bob Strong/AFP/Getty Images; p. 36 AFP/Getty Images; p. 39 (left) Courtesy of Robesus, Inc.; p. 40 Wikipedia.

Designer: Les Kanturek; Photo Researcher: Amy Feinberg